"BRING THE CLASSICS TO LIFE"

THE WAR
OF THE WORLDS

LEVEL 3

Series Designer
Philip J. Solimene

Editor
Laura Machynski

EDCON

Long Island, New York

Story Adaptor
Deborah Tiersch-Allen

Author
H. G. Wells

About the Author

Herbert George Wells was born on September 21, 1866, in Kent, England. His father, Joseph, owned a china and glass shop. He was also a professional bowler and coach for the Kent County Cricket Club. Joseph had an accident in 1877 which ended his professional career. This accident caused financial hardship for the family, and it was this tragedy that helped the Wells' marriage to fail. These difficulties forced young Herbert to leave school and make his own way in the world. He held many apprenticeships, but he believed in self-education. In his spare time he studied physiography, physiology, chemistry, and mathematics. In 1884, Herbert successfully obtained a scholarship to the Normal School of Science where he trained as a science teacher. It was here that he became editor of the school's journal where his first serious attempts at writing were published. In 1895, Wells opted for a full-time writing career and his first important short stories were published. His next work, *THE TIME MACHINE*, received 'rave' reviews and thereafter, his popularity grew as a writer of science fiction. Some of his other works include *THE ISLAND OF DR. MOREAU, WAR OF THE WORLDS,* and *THE FIRST MEN IN THE MOON.* H. G. Wells died in 1946. He left behind many works filled with wonder and fascination.

Copyright © 1993
A/V Concepts Corp.
Long Island, New York

Printed in U.S.A.
ISBN# 1-55576-097-X

CONTENTS

Words Used 4, 5

WORDS USED

Story 51	Story 52	Story 53	Story 54	Story 55
KEY WORDS				
earth	alarm	body	crash	event
flame	Friday	cart	dawn	Monday
smoke	heat	dead	direction	power
space	puff	huge	hundred	probably
upon	ugly	metal	meal	repair
war	weight	tower	women	Sunday
NECESSARY WORDS				
Mars	soldiers	thunder		destroyed
Martians				
meteorite				

WORDS USED

Story 56	Story 57	Story 58	Story 59	Story 60
		KEY WORDS		
cloud	blood	blade	ant	alive
coast	discover	careless	dream	bent
courage	dust	cause	inn	cousin
pale	fifth	throat	lonely	sick
ship	spider	wall	none	thin
travel	stiff	weep	tunnel	wreck
		NECESSARY WORDS		
carriage	brain	companion	germs	groceries

The Thing From Mars

PREPARATION

Key Words

earth	(ėrth)	our whole world; the giant ball of rock and water that we live on *People flew to the moon from <u>Earth</u>.*
flame	(flām)	the bright part of a fire *The fire burned with a red and yellow <u>flame</u>.*
smoke	(smōk)	what you see in the air when something burns *Black <u>smoke</u> came from the burning building.*
space	(spās)	everything outside our own world; an empty place *You need a special suit to take a trip through <u>space</u>.*
upon	(ə pôn´, ə pon´)	on *He put the ring <u>upon</u> his finger.*
war	(wôr)	a fight, often between armies *Our country went to <u>war</u> because we wanted to be free.*

The Thing From Mars

Necessary Words

Mars   (märz)   another world, like our Earth, that moves around the sun
> *You can sometimes see <u>Mars</u> as a bright point of light in the sky at night.*

Martians   (mär´ shənz)   being that are said to live on Mars
> *We know that there are no real <u>Martians</u>.*

meterorite   (mē´ tē ə rīt´)   something that falls to Earth from space
> *The <u>meteorite</u> looked like a big piece of rock.*

People

Ogilvy   is a friend of the man who is telling the story.

The Thing From Mars

No one knew the terrible thing that was heading toward Earth.

Preview: 1. Read the name of the story.
2. Look at the picture.
3. Read the sentence under the picture.
4. Read the first two paragraphs of the story.
5. Then answer the following question.

You learned from your preview that the author and his friend Ogilvy noticed a bright flame on Mars for
___ a. three nights.
___ b. four nights.
___ c. ten nights.
___ d. six nights.

Turn to the Comprehension Check on page 10 for the right answer.

Now read the story.

Read to find out what falls to Earth from the sky.

The Thing From Mars

No one would have believed in the last years of the 1800's, that someone was watching us. Surely, we on Earth did not know it. We did not even believe there was life on Mars. From far away, the Martians were watching us and making their plans.

It was six years ago that the war came upon us. One night my friend Ogilvy and I noticed a bright flame on Mars. Many others saw it, too. The next night there was another flame, and the next night another. Each night for ten nights we saw the same strange kind of flame. Nobody knew what it was. We did not know the terrible thing that was heading toward us through the darkness of space. It was already on its way, and it was getting nearer all the time.

One night I went for a walk with my wife. As we looked at the sky, I pointed out Mars to her. Many people were watching it and wondering what the flames might be. But we felt safe and had no thought of war.

Then came the night of the first falling flame. It was seen early in the morning, a line of green fire across the sky. I was writing near my window, yet I did not see this strange thing that came to Earth from space.

Ogilvy had seen the flame and thought it was a meteorite. He got up early with the idea of finding it. Find it he did, in a deep hole it had made when it landed. The grass near it was on fire, and blue smoke climbed toward the sky.

The Thing itself was very large. Ogilvy could see only part of it, but he was surprised at how large it was. He was also surprised to see that it was long and round, like a giant tree trunk. He had never seen a meteorite like this before.

Then he saw that the top of the Thing was beginning to move. He heard a strange sound. The end was turning like the top of a bottle. Something inside was opening the top!

"Good heavens!" said Ogilvy. "There's someone in it, trying to escape!" With a sudden flash, he got the idea that the Thing had something to do with the flame on Mars.

Wild with excitement, Ogilvy ran toward town to tell what he had found. At a little before nine that morning, I heard from my newspaper boy about the "men from Mars." I was startled and lost no time in getting to the scene.

I found a crowd of people around the hole in which the Thing lay. The top had stopped turning. I went closer to it and saw that the color was not like any on Earth. I felt sure that the Thing had come from Mars, but I did not think there was any living thing inside. After a while, as nothing seemed to be happening, I went home.

The newspaper that afternoon said this:

A MESSAGE
RECEIVED FROM MARS

Later I returned to the scene to find some men in the hole with the Thing. A bit of smoke still came from the grass. One of the men called, "Keep back!" The top of the Thing was turning again.

Then the top fell upon the ground with a ringing sound. I think everyone imagined we would see a man, or something more or less like a man. But what appeared was a round gray thing about as big as a bear. It had a kind of open mouth, like a V, with many long arms waving around it. It was the most terrible and frightening thing I had ever seen.

When another one began to climb out, I turned and ran madly. But then I stopped. Hiding in some bushes, I waited to see what would happen next.

The Thing From Mars

COMPREHENSION CHECK

Choose the best answer.

Preview Answer:

c. ten nights.

1. This story takes place in the last years of the
   ___a. 1800's.
   ___b. 1700's.
   ___c. 1600's.
   ___d. 1500's.

2. No one on Earth
   ___a. saw the flames on Mars.
   ___b. ever looked up at the sky.
   ___c. believed in Mars.
   ___d. believed there was life on Mars.

3. The first falling flame was seen
   ___a. in the early evening.
   ___b. in the early morning.
   ___c. late at night.
   ___d. at dinner time.

4. When the first flame came to Earth
   ___a. it made a lot of noise.
   ___b. it landed quietly.
   ___c. it made a deep hole in the ground.
   ___d. it made a soft landing.

5. Ogilvy thought the flame that landed
   ___a. was a meteorite.
   ___b. was an airplane.
   ___c. was a machine from space.
   ___d. was a burning tree branch.

6. When Ogilvy saw the top of the Thing opening up,
   ___a. he ran home to tell his wife.
   ___b. he ran home to tell his mother.
   ___c. he ran back to town to tell everyone.
   ___d. he left the country.

7. The newspaper story
   ___a. sent many curious people to the crash scene.
   ___b. caused many people to leave town.
   ___c. made everyone laugh.
   ___d. was believed by no one.

8. The things that came climbing out of the craft were
   ___a. friendly looking.
   ___b. very frightening.
   ___c. very small.
   ___d. nice to look at.

9. Another name for this story could be
   ___a. "A Strange Kind of Dream."
   ___b. "Our Friends From Mars."
   ___c. "The Martians Have Landed."
   ___d. "Flames in the Sky."

10. This story is mainly about
   ___a. other beings that have come to Earth from space.
   ___b. a good newspaper story.
   ___c. flames falling from the sky.
   ___d. life on Mars.

Check your answers with the key on page 67.

This page may be reproduced for classroom use.

The Thing From Mars

VOCABULARY CHECK

earth	flame	smoke	space	upon	war

I. Sentences to Finish

Fill in the blank in each sentence with the correct key word from the box above.

1. I saw a _____ of light coming from the house across the street.

2. All people on _____ need water to live.

3. When I saw _____ coming from the building, I called the police.

4. The crown was placed _____ the king's head.

5. My father joined the Army and went to _____.

6. Men travel through _____ to reach the moon.

II. Making Sense of Sentences

Put a check next to YES if the sentence makes sense. Put a check next to NO if the sentence does not make sense.

1. The <u>Earth</u> is made up of milk and cheese. _____ YES _____ NO

2. When something burns, <u>smoke</u> rises up in the air. _____ YES _____ NO

3. If I put a book <u>upon</u> the table, I put it under the table. _____ YES _____ NO

4. Friends make <u>war</u> all the time. _____ YES _____ NO

5. You must travel through <u>space</u> to reach the moon. _____ YES _____ NO

6. If you pour water on a <u>flame</u> it goes out. _____ YES _____ NO

Check your answers with the key on page 69.

This page may be reproduced for classroom use.

Friday Night

PREPARATION

Key Words

alarm	(ə lärm´)	fear *The driver's <u>alarm</u> grew as the snow fell faster.*
Friday	(frī´ dē, frī´ dā)	a day of the week *<u>Friday</u> is the last day of the school week.*
heat	(hēt)	what is felt when it is hot *You can feel the <u>heat</u> when the oven is on.*
puff	(puf)	a quick sending out of air or smoke *A <u>puff</u> of smoke came from the chimney.*
ugly	(ug´ lē)	not pleasing to look at *Some people think frogs are <u>ugly</u>.*
weight	(wāt)	how heavy a thing is *The <u>weight</u> of the box broke the table.*

Friday Night

Necessary Words

soldiers   (sōl´jərs)   people who are in an army
The <u>soldiers</u> put down their guns.

Friday Night

My neighbor and I watch to see what the ugly things are up to.

Preview: 1. Read the name of the story.
2. Look at the picture.
3. Read the sentence under the picture.
4. Read the first paragraph of the story.
5. Then answer the following question.

You learned from your preview that the author was
___ a. an ugly man.
___ b. a good-looking man.
___ c. a curious person.
___ d. a coward.

Turn to the Comprehension Check on page 16 for the right answer.

Now read the story.

Read to find out why everyone's excitement turns to alarm.

Friday Night

I did not dare go back to the hole, but I was curious to see what was happening. As I tried to find a safe place to hide and watch, I met a neighbor. "What ugly things!" he said. He kept saying this over and over.

Toward evening, a group of men appeared at the edge of the hole. They waved a white flag to show that they were friendly. From the hole came a puff of green smoke. There was another puff, and then another. Then came a white flame and a blinding flash of light. The heat was so great that the trees were set on fire. The men fell to the ground and did not move again. A terrible fear came over me. I turned and ran, not daring to look back.

Somehow I made my way home. My wife was startled by how awful I looked. I told her about the Martians and the heat guns they used to kill the men. Her feeling of alarm showed on her face. "They may come here," she said again and again.

I explained that the ugly things could hardly move. On Earth, the Martians must weigh three times what they would weigh on Mars. Their own weight would keep them from getting out of the deep hole they were in.

"They may stay in the hole and kill those that come near," I said. "But they cannot get out of it."

There was one thing I had not thought about. The Martians had made a machine that flew to Earth. If they also had a machine to carry them on land, their weight would not matter.

That day was Friday. I did not believe then that the Martians had been foolish. I was feeling better as I sat down to eat. I remember my dear wife's face and how nice the table looked. I did not know it, but that was the last good dinner I was to eat for many strange and terrible days.

Everyone was talking about the Martians, but with little sense of alarm. The newspapers believed, as I did, that the Martians' own weight would keep them from escaping the hole. People stayed away from that place. But some said they could hear a sound coming from there. It sounded like the noise of hammers.

So that is how things were on Friday night. Here was this Thing sticking into the skin of our Earth. There was fear and excitement in the streets and homes of our town. Farther away, life went on as it always had. The war had not yet begun.

All night long the Martians hammered, at work on the machines they were making. From time to time a puff of green or white smoke climbed slowly into the sky.

Late that night, some soldiers came to our town. They spoke to people in the streets and asked them questions. I was glad to see that the Army thought this might be a serious matter.

In the middle of the night, the crowd on the street saw something fall from the sky. It was green in color and made a bright fire as it fell to Earth. This was the second Thing from Mars.

15

Friday Night

COMPREHENSION CHECK

Choose the best answer.

1. A group of men appeared at the hole waving
   ___a. a green flag.
   ___b. a white flag.
   ___c. a red flag.
   ___d. their hands.

2. The flag was waved to show the Martians that they were
   ___a. friendly men.
   ___b. angry men.
   ___c. ready for war.
   ___d. ready for dinner.

3. From the hole came three puffs of green smoke, then a blinding flash of light. The heat was so great that
   ___a. everyone went to the beach.
   ___b. the men became very thirsty.
   ___c. it killed the men.
   ___d. the whole town was set on fire.

4. The blinding flash of light came from
   ___a. a flashlight.
   ___b. a sun lamp.
   ___c. a fire ball.
   ___d. a heat gun.

5. The author explained to his wife that the ugly things
   ___a. were nothing to worry about.
   ___b. were trying to be friendly.
   ___c. were stuck in the mud.
   ___d. were too heavy to get out of the hole they were in.

6. The Martians hammered all through the night. They were
   ___a. building another spaceship.
   ___b. hanging up pictures.
   ___c. making some kind of machines.
   ___d. trying to keep everyone awake.

7. The Army came into town because
   ___a. the Martians were a danger to the people.
   ___b. a war with the Martians had begun.
   ___c. they were ordered to take pictures.
   ___d. they had never seen a spaceship.

8. Late Friday Night
   ___a. the Martians returned home.
   ___b. the Martians stopped working on their machines.
   ___c. a fire broke out in the town.
   ___d. a second Thing fell from Mars to Earth.

9. Another name for this story could be
   ___a. "The Strangers From Space."
   ___b. "The World On Fire."
   ___c. "Big Fat Martians."
   ___d. "Foolish Martians."

10. This story is mainly about
    ___a. why the Martians didn't come out of their hole.
    ___b. why a town's excitement turns to fear.
    ___c. how the Army will fight the Martians.
    ___d. a group of men who were killed by a heat gun.

Check your answers with the key on page 67.

Friday Night

VOCABULARY CHECK

| alarm | Friday | heat | puff | ugly | weight |

I. Sentences to Finish

Fill in the blank in each sentence with the correct key word from the box above.

1. My dog's _____ is about sixty pounds.

2. My friend and I go to see a show every _____ night.

3. The _____ from the fire kept the firemen from entering the building.

4. A _____ of wind blew the man's hat off.

5. Mother showed _____ when Dad did not show up for dinner.

6. The _____ giant loved the beautiful princess.

II. Matching

Write the letter of the correct meaning from Column B next to the key word in Column A.

Column A

_____ 1. puff

_____ 2. heat

_____ 3. Friday

_____ 4. alarm

_____ 5. ugly

_____ 6. weight

Column B

a. how heavy a thing is

b. fear

c. not pleasing to look at

d. a day of the week

e. a quick sending out of air or smoke

f. what is felt when it is hot

Check your answers with the key on page 69.

THE WAR BEGINS

PREPARATION

Key Words

body	(bod´ē)	the part of someone that is not the head or legs *A coat keeps your <u>body</u> warm.*
cart	(kärt)	small wagon *The pony pulled a little <u>cart</u>.*
dead	(ded)	not living *The hunter carried two <u>dead</u> birds.*
huge	(hyüj)	very large *A whale is a <u>huge</u> animal.*
metal	(met´l)	what many hard, shiny things are made of *Gold is a <u>metal</u>; so is iron.*
tower	(tou´ər)	tall building or part of a building *The round stone <u>tower</u> could be seen from far away.*

THE WAR BEGINS

Necessary Words

thunder (thun´dər) the loud noise which often follows a flash of lightning
During the storm, the <u>thunder</u> got so loud that I had to cover my ears.

THE WAR BEGINS

The soldiers asked me many questions.
I told them about the Martians' special guns.

Preview:
1. Read the name of the story.
2. Look at the picture.
3. Read the sentences under the picture.
4. Read the first two paragraphs of the story.
5. Then answer the following question.

You learned from your preview that the Martians had killed some men with
___ a. their heat guns.
___ b. their hot guns.
___ c. a strange light.
___ d. a flag.

Turn to the Comprehension Check on page 22 for the right answer.

Now read the story.

Read to find out how the soldiers prepare to fight the Martians.

THE WAR BEGINS

On Saturday morning I saw my neighbor outside. He told me about a fire in the woods. "They say another one of those things from Mars fell there," he said, pointing.

After breakfast, I took a walk and met some soldiers. They had not yet seen the Martians, so they asked me many questions. I told them about the strange light and the Martians' heat guns. The men who had gone to the hole with the flag were dead. My friend Ogilvy was one of them. Yet, as I talked to the soldiers, I still believed the Martians had no chance to win. I didn't even think it would be a fair fight.

During the afternoon, the soldiers put big guns in place near both of the Things that had come from Mars. At about six in the evening, I was sitting with my wife when we heard a terrible sound, like thunder. Running out, I saw the trees in flames. The tower of the church fell to the ground, and our own chimney was broken. My wife and I stood there, amazed. Then the thought came to me that our house was now in reach of the Martians' heat guns.

"We can't stay here," I said. I decided we must go to my wife's family, who lived about twelve miles away. We needed some way to get there, so I went quickly to get a cart and horse. As we were packing a few things in the cart, a soldier came running up. He was going from house to house warning people to leave. I shouted after him, "What is going on?"

He turned, stared, and called out something about "crawling out in a thing like a dish cover." Then he hurried on.

We got safely to the home of my wife's family. I had some dinner and gave the horse a rest. It was late when I left my wife there and started for home, planning to return the horse and cart to their owner. On the way, I saw a line of green fire fall through the sky. It was the third Thing from Mars!

As I got nearer to home, a giant storm began. Then, in a flash of light, I saw a thing that amazed me. It was huge; taller than many houses, and it had three legs. It walked right over the trees, knocking them to the ground. I could see that it must be some kind of machine, for it was made of metal.

Then suddenly, out of the trees ahead of me, a second huge machine appeared. It seemed to be rushing straight toward me. I pulled the horse's head hard to the right. The cart turned over, and I ended up in a puddle. A moment later, the machine went walking by me.

Up close, the thing looked even more strange. It had long arms like metal ropes swinging from its body. At the top was a kind of metal head that moved from side to side, as if the thing was looking around. Puffs of green smoke came from the huge body.

After the two machines were gone, I got up and started toward my house. On the way, I tripped over the body of a man in the road. It was the owner of the cart and horse, and he was dead.

I finally got to my house. In the garden, I met a soldier and asked him to come in. He told me he had seen the Martians crawl out of the hole under a metal dish. Then the metal dish stood up on three huge legs, the first of the fighting machines I had seen.

As the sun came up, we looked out the window. Every tower and many homes had fallen, and smoke was everywhere. Three of the shining machines were working at the hole, which looked larger now than it had before.

THE WAR BEGINS

COMPREHENSION CHECK

Choose the best answer.

1. The second Thing that fell from Mars to Earth caused
   ___a. a great flood.
   ___b. a fire in the woods.
   ___c. the earth to shake.
   ___d. mud slides.

2. The author's friend Ogilvy
   ___a. tried to kill the Martians.
   ___b. left the country.
   ___c. was killed crossing a busy street.
   ___d. was killed by the Martians' heat guns.

3. The soldiers and the Martians began fighting around
   ___a. four o'clock.
   ___b. five o'clock.
   ___c. six o'clock.
   ___d. seven o'clock.

4. The author, fearing for his wife's safety, brought her to
   ___a. her family about twelve miles away.
   ___b. a hospital.
   ___c. a church.
   ___d. a neighbor's house.

5. After leaving his wife with her family, the author headed back home. As he got nearer to home,
   ___a. a giant storm began.
   ___b. it began to snow.
   ___c. he saw his house on fire.
   ___d. he was shot with a heat gun.

6. In a flash of light the author caught sight of a huge machine with three legs. This flash of light was
   ___a. a car's headlights.
   ___b. a truck's headlights.
   ___c. a flashlight.
   ___d. lightning.

7. The strange-looking machines were called
   ___a. giants.
   ___b. puppets.
   ___c. metal movers.
   ___d. fighting machines.

8. The Martians
   ___a. never came out of their hole.
   ___b. were inside of the fighting machines.
   ___c. knew that coming to Earth was a mistake.
   ___d. ate their food off of metal dishes.

9. Another name for this story could be
   ___a. "War Machines."
   ___b. "Run For Your Life!"
   ___c. "Our Friends From Mars."
   ___d. "Trouble For Ogilvy."

10. This story is mainly about
    ___a. a town on fire.
    ___b. how Ogilvy died.
    ___c. the Martians beginning their attack on Earth.
    ___d. the Martians' friendly visit.

Check your answers with the key on page 67.

THE WAR BEGINS

VOCABULARY CHECK

body	cart	dead	huge	metal	tower

I. Sentences to Finish

Fill in the blank in each sentence with the correct key word from the box above.

1. Mother washes the baby's _____ in a small tub.

2. Dad bought me a set of _____ cars for my birthday.

3. The king looked out the _____ window at the crowd below.

4. The baby elephant looked like a mouse next to its _____ mother.

5. The flowers were _____ because no one watered them.

6. The farmer filled his _____ with corn and headed for market.

II. Boxed-In Words

Use the words from the box above to write the words that go with each meaning. Then use the letters in the shaded boxes to solve the riddle.

1. very large

2. a small wagon

3. a tall building or part of a building

4. not living

5. what many hard, shiny things are made of

6. the part of someone that is not the hands or legs

CLUE: Please speak up, I can _____ hear you.

ANSWER: _____ _____ _____ _____ _____ _____

Check your answers with the key on page 69.

This page may be reproduced for classroom use.

A Terrible Fight

PREPARATION

Key Words

crash	(krash)	a loud noise *We heard the <u>crash</u> when the tree fell.*
dawn	(dôn)	the first light in the morning *The birds began to sing at <u>dawn</u>.*
direction	(də rek´ shən, dī rek´ shən)	the way one must go to get to a certain place *What <u>direction</u> should I walk in to get to your house?*
hundred	(hun´ drəd)	a number; 100 *It takes one <u>hundred</u> pennies to make a dollar.*
meal	(mel)	breakfast, lunch, or dinner *They sat at the kitchen table to eat their <u>meal</u>.*
women	(wim´ ən)	more than one woman *Her mother and grandmother are both strong <u>women</u>.*

A Terrible Fight

Necessary Words

Places

London   a city in England

A Terrible Fight

Knowing we are in great danger, the soldier and I get ready to leave the house.

Preview:
1. Read the name of the story.
2. Look at the picture.
3. Read the sentence under the picture.
4. Read the first paragraph of the story.
5. Then answer the following question.

You learned from your preview that the author's house
___ a. was not a safe place to stay.
___ b. was a safe place to be.
___ c. was being attacked by the Martians.
___ d. was full of food.

Turn to the Comprehension Check on page 28 for the right answer.

Now read the story.

Read to find out what happens as the author makes his way toward London.

A Terrible Fight

As dawn came and the sky grew bright, the soldier and I left the window. We both knew that my house was not a safe place to stay. The soldier wanted to head in the direction of London. He hoped to join his soldier friends there. My plan was to get my wife and leave the country with her. From what I had seen of the Martians so far, I understood that we were all in great danger.

Between me and the place where my wife was, lay the third Thing from Mars, and the metal giants who guarded it. I would have to go in a different direction to get around it. I was ready to leave right then, soon after dawn, but the soldier knew better. In times of war, he said, it can be hard to get a meal. He and I both filled our pockets with food. Then we crept out of the house. There was nobody around and all was silent, even the birds.

After a time, we met three soldiers on horses. The soldier who was with me was eager to talk to them. Their captain asked what the Martians were like.

"Metal giants, sir," my friend said. "One hundred feet high. Three legs and a metal body and a great huge head, sir."

The captain did not believe him.

"You'll see, sir," said my friend. "They carry a kind of box that shoots fire. Trees and houses fall with a crash, and people die, sir." I could see that the other soldiers still did not believe him.

"It's all true," I said.

We went on our way. Farther along we saw three women and two children. They were busy putting things from their house into a cart, in a great hurry to get away.

After a while, the soldier and I sat down to rest. The food we had in our pockets made a very good meal.

In the next town, we found a crowd of more than one hundred men and women. They were also packing wagons and carts. They knew the town might be attacked, and they wanted to get out of there. But they felt sure the Martians would lose in a fight with the soldiers.

We were near the river when we heard the sound of guns. The fight was beginning. Quickly, one after the other, one, two, three, four of the metal giants appeared. And, from another direction, there came number five. It held up its terrible heat gun.

"Get under water!" I shouted. I splashed into the river, and so did most of the others. When I looked up, I saw one of the Martians very near. All at once, the soldiers who had been hiding there shot at the machine. The head blew right off, and bits of metal fell to the ground.

The machine kept going, knocking over trees and buildings. At last, it fell with a huge crash into the river. Water, mud, and metal shot into the air.

Then the other machines attacked with their heat guns. The air was filled with smoke and noise, and the water of the river got so hot that I screamed. I remember the foot of a metal giant near me. I don't know how I escaped. I just know I was very, very lucky.

Now I began to make my way toward London. Along the way, I met a man who did little but cry and complain. As the moon came up, we could hear guns from across the water. "We had better go this way," I said. And so we went on together.

27

A Terrible Fight

COMPREHENSION CHECK

Choose the best answer.

1. The soldier wanted to head toward London. The author wanted to get his wife and
    ___a. go out for dinner.
    ___b. go shopping.
    ___c. leave the neighborhood.
    ___d. leave the country.

2. The soldier told the author not to go anywhere
    ___a. without him.
    ___b. without food.
    ___c. without a gun.
    ___d. without money.

3. After a time, the author and the soldier met three soldiers who
    ___a. had no food or water.
    ___b. were not armed.
    ___c. had not yet seen the Martians.
    ___d. had not heard about the Martians.

4. When the soldiers were told what the Martians looked like, and about the box they carried,
    ___a. they did not believe it.
    ___b. they left town.
    ___c. they laughed real hard.
    ___d. they became very frightened.

5. Many people were packing their belongings and leaving town because
    ___a. their houses had all been burned.
    ___b. it was the time of year for vacation.
    ___c. their lives were in danger.
    ___d. all the stores in town were closed.

6. The Martians' heat guns
    ___a. made things burn up.
    ___b. left puddles of water everywhere.
    ___c. only worked at night.
    ___d. were useful toys.

7. The author went under water to get out of the heat gun's path. But he screamed when
    ___a. he saw a large fish swimming his way.
    ___b. he heard the sound of a large ship coming toward him.
    ___c. the water began to freeze.
    ___d. the water got very hot.

8. With all the things that were happening, the author
    ___a. was glad to be alive.
    ___b. felt sorry for the Martians.
    ___c. was able to sleep well.
    ___d. was not worried for his own safety.

9. Another name for this story could be
    ___a. "A Country Without Food."
    ___b. "At War with the Metal Giants."
    ___c. "Guns By the River."
    ___d. "The Town that Ran Away."

10. This story is mainly about
    ___a. how hard it is to find food during war time.
    ___b. a box that shoots fire.
    ___c. people hurrying to leave a country that is at war with Martians.
    ___d. soldiers that were not able to win the war.

Check your answers with the key on page 67.

This page may be reproduced for classroom use.

A Terrible Fight

VOCABULARY CHECK

crash	dawn	direction	hundred	meal	women

I. Sentences to Finish

Fill in the blank in each sentence with the correct key word from the box above.

1. The plane fell from the sky and landed with a _____ .

2. We awake before _____ to get ready for our fishing trip.

3. It takes one _____ nickels to make five dollars.

4. Our family eats a big _____ on Thanksgiving Day.

5. The _____ of the church are planning a picnic.

6. I thought I was headed in the right _____ , but I got lost.

II. Crossword Puzzle

Fill in the boxes in the puzzle with the correct key words from the box above. The clues will help you choose the correct word.

Across

1. a number; 100
2. more than one woman
3. a loud noise

Down

1. the first light in the morning
2. the way one must go to get to a certain place
3. breakfast, lunch, or dinner

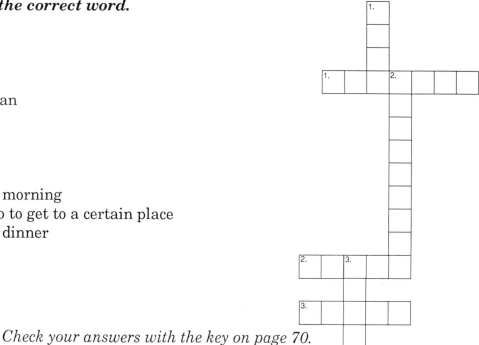

Check your answers with the key on page 70.

The Black Smoke

PREPARATION

Key Words

event	(i vent´)	something that happens
		The party was an <u>event</u> that everyone enjoyed.
Monday	(mun´ de, mun´ dā)	a day of the week
		The school week begins on <u>Monday</u>.
power	(pou´ ər)	what things or people have when they are strong
		The <u>power</u> of the wind was so great that a big tree was knocked down.
probably	(prob´ ə blē)	pretty sure to happen
		The sky is so dark it will <u>probably</u> rain.
repair	(ri per´; ri par´)	fix; set right
		I hope he will be able to <u>repair</u> the broken wheel on my bicycle.
Sunday	(sun´ de, sun´ dā)	a day of the week
		We went to my grandmother's house on <u>Sunday</u>.

The Black Smoke

Necessary Words

destroyed   (di stroi´ əd)   ruined; had put an end to; killed
The fire <u>destroyed</u> our neighbor's house.

The Black Smoke

At the station, my brother finds that the train is not running.
Could the Martians have something to do with this?

Preview:	1. Read the name of the story.
	2. Look at the picture.
	3. Read the sentences under the picture.
	4. Read the first five paragraphs of the story.
	5. Then answer the following question.

You learned from your preview that the author's brother
___ a. wanted to kill the Martians.
___ b. wanted to see the Martians before they went back to Mars.
___ c. wanted to see the Martians before they were destroyed.
___ d. had gone mad.

Turn to the Comprehension Check on page 34 for the right answer.

Now read the story.

Read to find out how the Martians fight the soldiers.

The Black Smoke

My brother was in London when the Martians came to Earth. On Saturday, he read that they were still in their hole. The newspaper said they were probably too heavy to get out.

Reading that, my brother did not worry about my wife and me. But he decided to come down that night to visit us. He said he wanted to see the Martians before they were destroyed.

When he got to the station, he found that the train was not running. No one seemed to know why. Few people thought it had anything to do with the Martians.

By late in the day on Sunday, my brother heard news of the event at the river. That helped him to understand the power of the Martians. Now he did begin to worry.

Early Monday morning, my brother woke up to the sounds of bells ringing and feet running in the streets. At first he thought the world had probably gone mad. Outside his window he heard someone calling, "They're coming! The Martians are coming!"

That was the dawn of the great fear. London had gone to bed Sunday night feeling safe. On Monday morning, the city woke to a strong sense of danger.

In the streets, voices were crying, "Black smoke! Black smoke!" My brother soon found out that the Martians were headed for London. And now they were shooting out a kind of black smoke that killed everyone it touched. My brother took all of his money and went outside.

We found out later that three of the Martians had come out of their hole Sunday night. Soldiers shot at them, and one of the metal machines fell. The Martian kept making a loud noise until the other two came to help it.

Those who saw the event said that one of the machine's legs was broken. The Martian inside crawled out. It seemed to be trying to repair the leg. The other Martians stood guard. It seemed that the Martian did repair the leg, for soon the machine was up and walking again.

A bit later, four more Martians joined these three. Each of them carried a strange black bundle. They gave some of the black things to the other Martians. Then the seven of them spread out and began to move forward.

I was walking along the road with the man I had met, when two of the machines suddenly appeared. We found a place to hide and watch. Ahead of the Martians, soldiers were waiting with their guns. I wondered what the Martians thought of us. Did they know that we on Earth could make plans and work together?

Then one of the Martians shot something from a black bundle it carried. There was no flash, no smoke. But the ground shook from the power of the shot. More shots like it followed. Things like huge cans fell to the ground and broke open. From them a heavy black smoke began to spread in all directions.

As the black smoke rolled over the soldiers, their guns fell silent. There was no way to escape this terrible smoke. At about this same time, the fourth Thing from Mars fell through space to land on Earth.

After Sunday night, the soldiers no longer tried to fight the Martians. The only wise thing to do was to get as far away from them as possible.

The Black Smoke

COMPREHENSION CHECK

Choose the best answer.

1. The author's brother lived
   ___a. on Mars.
   ___b. in London.
   ___c. in Largo.
   ___d. in a hole.

2. When he got to the train station, he found
   ___a. his brother and his wife.
   ___b. Martians.
   ___c. that the train was not running.
   ___d. that the train had already left.

3. When he heard what had happened at the river, the author's brother
   ___a. didn't believe the story.
   ___b. became worried.
   ___c. decided not to visit his brother.
   ___d. went to the store to buy another newspaper.

4. The people of London became mad with fear when they learned that
   ___a. the Martians were headed for London.
   ___b. the trains weren't running any more.
   ___c. there wasn't enough food in London to feed its people.
   ___d. the river had dried up.

5. The Martians were shooting out a kind of black smoke that
   ___a. had a nice smell.
   ___b. dried up all the rivers.
   ___c. killed everyone who saw it.
   ___d. killed everyone it touched.

6. The black smoke came from
   ___a. the Martians' hole.
   ___b. the sky.
   ___c. red bundles that the Martians carried.
   ___d. huge cans that the Martians shot from a black bundle.

7. The Martians inside the metal giants were able to make repairs to the machines
   ___a. quickly.
   ___b. within hours.
   ___c. within days.
   ___d. within weeks.

8. When the Martians shot the black smoke,
   ___a. all living things died.
   ___b. the ground melted.
   ___c. the ground shook.
   ___d. it started to rain.

9. Another name for this story could be
   ___a. "A Great Fear in London."
   ___b. "Silent Guns."
   ___c. "A Mad, Mad, World."
   ___d. "A City Sleeps."

10. This story is mainly about
   ___a. how the Martians traveled to London.
   ___b. why it's important to read the newspapers.
   ___c. why the soldiers wouldn't fight the Martians.
   ___d. the great power the Martians had over the people on Earth.

Check your answers with the key on page 67.

This page may be reproduced for classroom use.

The Black Smoke

VOCABULARY CHECK

| event | Monday | power | probably | repair | Sunday |

I. Sentences to Finish

Fill in the blank in each sentence with the correct key word from the box above.

1. Dad works Monday through Saturday. He is off on _____ .

2. The _____ of the storm blew off our roof.

3. Father will _____ the broken fence.

4. The circus is a big _____ in our small town.

5. We will _____ go out to eat because Mother burned the dinner.

6. The school week begins on _____ and ends on Friday.

II. Using the Words

On the lines below, write six of your own sentences using the key words from the box above. Use each word once, drawing a line under the key word.

1. _____

2. _____

3. _____

4. _____

5. _____

6. _____

Check your answers with the key on page 70.

This page may be reproduced for classroom use.

My Brother's Escape

PREPARATION

Key Words

cloud	(kloud)	thing in the air made of many tiny drops of water *There was just one white <u>cloud</u> in the blue sky.*
coast	(kōst)	land at the edge of the sea *During the storm, big waves washed up all along the <u>coast</u>.*
courage	(kėr´ ij)	what brave people have *It takes a lot of <u>courage</u> to fight fires.*
pale	(pāl)	lighter in color than one should be *Fear sometimes makes people turn <u>pale</u>.*
ship	(ship)	large boat *We watched the <u>ship</u> until it was far out at sea.*
travel	(trav´ əl)	to take a trip *Did you ever <u>travel</u> by airplane?*

My Brother's Escape

Necessary Words

carriage   (kar´ ij)   something people ride in
                                          Four horses pulled the <u>carriage</u>.

People

Miss Elphinstone   is a young woman trying to get out of London.

Mrs. Elphinstone   is the wife of Miss Elphinstone's brother.

My Brother's Escape

Hearing the screams of two women, my brother runs to help them.

Preview:
1. Read the name of the story.
2. Look at the picture.
3. Read the sentence under the picture.
4. Read the first two paragraphs of the story.
5. Then answer the following question.

You learned from your preview that the people of London
___ a. were trying to get away.
___ b. were preparing to fight the Martians.
___ c. did not like to ride trains.
___ d. only liked to ride bicycles.

Turn to the Comprehension Check on page 40 for the right answer.

Now read the story.

Read to find out how the author's brother gets away.

My Brother's Escape

By Monday a great wave of fear had rolled through London. Trains filled with people left the city and did not return. My brother could not get a place on a train. But he was lucky enough to find a bicycle. So he was able to travel out of London.

After a while, a wheel of the bicycle broke. My brother was on foot when he heard the screams of two women. Three men were pulling them out of their small carriage. My brother ran to help. As he struggled with the men, the women began to drive away.

My brother would probably not have had a chance to win. But the younger woman showed great courage. She turned the carriage around and took a small gun from under the seat. She fired the gun, and the men ran.

Now the two women decided to let my brother travel with them. Soon the road was crowded with more and more people, carts, and carriages. My brother saw a cloud of gray smoke ahead of them.

"What is this you are driving us into?" cried Mrs. Elphinstone, the older of the two women. The main road was like a sea of people. People with pale faces and wild eyes pushed and shouted. Cries and screams filled the air. A man fell and was run over by a horse and wagon.

At first, my brother and the two women turned back from the road. It just did not seem possible to go on that way. Both Mrs. Elphinstone and Miss Elphinstone were pale with fear. But my brother knew that their only hope of escape was to stay on the main road.

"We must go that way," he told Miss Elphinstone. Again she showed great courage, and somehow they were able to struggle on. My brother's plan was to get to the coast as quickly as possible. There he hoped they could find a ship to take them out of the country.

They spent many days and nights on the road. At last they reached the coast. They were already aboard a ship when three Martians appeared. My brother had not seen the Martians before, and he was astonished.

Suddenly a huge iron ship of war rushed past my brother's ship. It headed straight for one of the Martians. The Martian shot a can of black smoke, but the ship kept coming. It attacked the Martian, which fell with a giant splash.

My brother and the others cheered. Then, out of the cloud of smoke, they saw the ship of war again. Now it was speeding toward the second Martian. The Martian fired its heat gun. The ship was in flames, but still it rushed forward. Down went the second Martian.

Everyone was shouting and cheering. A cloud of smoke kept them from seeing anything more. My brother's ship headed away from the coast as fast as it could go.

The sun went down, and the sky began to grow dark. Suddenly, the captain of the ship cried out and pointed. Something rushed up into the sky above the clouds. It was very wide and large. And as it flew, it rained down darkness upon the land.

My Brother's Escape

COMPREHENSION CHECK

Choose the best answer.

1. The author's brother left London
   ___a. by train.
   ___b. by bicycle.
   ___c. on a horse.
   ___d. on foot.

2. When he heard two women screaming, the author's brother
   ___a. ran to help them.
   ___b. ran the other way.
   ___c. covered his ears.
   ___d. went to find the police.

3. The young woman showed great courage when
   ___a. she screamed.
   ___b. she shot the men with her gun.
   ___c. she drove away real fast.
   ___d. she turned the carriage around and went back to help the author's brother.

4. The two women wanted the author's brother to travel with them
   ___a. so they would have more company.
   ___b. because he could fix the carriage if it broke down.
   ___c. in case they ran into more trouble.
   ___d. because he was a fine-looking man.

5. The author's brother hoped to get to the coast and
   ___a. do some fishing.
   ___b. look for sea shells.
   ___c. find a ship to take them on vacation.
   ___d. find a ship to take them out of the country.

6. How long did it take before the three travelers reached the coast?
   ___a. Many days and nights
   ___b. Two weeks
   ___c. Four months
   ___d. One year

7. At the coast, what was it that attacked the Martians?
   ___a. A cloud of smoke
   ___b. A ship of war
   ___c. A small fishing boat
   ___d. An army of soldiers

8. When the ship attacked the Martians, the Martians fought back with
   ___a. baseball bats.
   ___b. bows and arrows.
   ___c. heat guns and red plants.
   ___d. heat guns and black smoke.

9. Another name for this story could be
   ___a. "A Sea of People."
   ___b. "A Young Woman of Courage."
   ___c. "Slow Boat to Nowhere."
   ___d. "Safe at Sea."

10. This story is mainly about
    ___a. a man who liked to ride trains.
    ___b. a man who liked to travel.
    ___c. how the people of London struggled to save themselves from the Martians.
    ___d. how the people of London fought bravely against the Martians.

Check your answers with the key on page 67.

This page may be reproduced for classroom use.

My Brother's Escape

VOCABULARY CHECK

cloud	coast	courage	pale	ship	travel

I. Sentences to Finish

Fill in the blank in each sentence with the correct key word from the box above.

1. We watched as the _____ pulled out to sea.

2. It was such a beautiful day; not a _____ in the sky.

3. I will _____ by car to visit my grandmother.

4. The man showed great _____ when he entered the bear's cave.

5. Bill turned _____ when he saw a lion inside his tent.

6. We were careful not to sail the boat along the rocky _____ .

II. Matching

Write the letter of the correct meaning from Column B next to the key word in Column A.

Column A		Column B
1. travel	_____	a. land at the edge of the sea
2. pale	_____	b. to take a trip
3. courage	_____	c. a large boat
4. coast	_____	d. lighter in color than one should be
5. ship	_____	e. thing in the air made of many tiny drops of water
6. cloud	_____	f. what brave people have

Check your answers with the key on page 70.

This page may be reproduced for classroom use.

More Martians

PREPARATION

Key Words

blood   (blud)   what runs through your body
When I cut my finger, some <u>blood</u> got on my clothes.

discover   (dis kuv´ ər)   find
What did you <u>discover</u> in the secret cave?

dust   (dust)   tiny bits that make things dirty
We cleaned the <u>dust</u> off the old books.

fifth   (fifth)   number five in a set
The first four days were sunny, but the <u>fifth</u> day it rained.

spider   (spī´ dər)   small animal with eight legs
I saw the <u>spider</u> catch a fly.

stiff   (stif)   hard to bend
The new shoes were a little <u>stiff</u>, but they soon got softer.

More Martians

Necessary Words

brain   (brān)   part of you that is inside your head
You use your <u>brain</u> to think.

More Martians

Outside, everything was covered with black dust.

Preview: 1. Read the name of the story.
2. Look at the picture.
3. Read the sentence under the picture.
4. Read the first five paragraphs of the story.
5. Then answer the following question.

You learned from your preview that the man in the house with the author was

___ a. a brave man.
___ b. a smart man.
___ c. a very helpful man.
___ d. a coward.

Turn to the Comprehension Check on page 46 for the right answer.

Now read the story.

Read to find out what happens when the fifth Thing falls from Mars.

More Martians

While my brother was escaping from London, I was in an empty house. The man I had met, the one who cried and complained, was still with me. We were hiding from the black smoke.

All Sunday night and all day Monday we stayed there. We had nothing to do but wait. I was very worried about my wife. And I soon grew tired of hearing the man with me complain. He was, I am sorry to say, selfish and a coward.

On Monday a Martian came across the fields. It did something to make the black smoke disappear. Late in the day, the idea came to me that now we could get away. But the man with me did not want to leave. "We are safe here," he kept saying.

I decided to go alone. I was glad to discover some food that I could take with me. Just as I was about to leave, the coward decided to come with me after all. I wish now that I had left him there, but I did not.

Outside, everything was covered with black dust. We walked for some hours and crossed a bridge over the river. On the other side, we saw more of the dust that the black smoke had left behind. Then, over the tops of the houses, we suddenly saw a Martian. If it looked down, it was sure to discover us. We quickly found a place to hide. There we stayed until the Martian was gone.

I was eager to get to my wife, so I started out again. The coward came hurrying after me. We had not gone far when we saw another Martian. Some people were running away from it. The Martian caught them, picked them up, and put them into a kind of metal basket on its back. I wondered what it was going to do with them.

At last we made our way to another house. Nobody was there, but they had left some food. We were eating bread and meat when we saw a flash of green light. Then there was a huge crash.

The next thing I remember was waking up with blood on my face. The floor was covered with broken glass. We heard a sound outside. It was a Martian!

At dawn we peeked out through a hole and saw what had happened. The fifth Thing from Mars had fallen. It had landed right beside the house where we were. Most of the house had been knocked down around us.

I could see that the Martian ship was already open. One of the metal fighting machines stood near it, stiff and tall. In the hole where the fifth Thing lay, I saw a new kind of machine. This one looked like a huge metal spider.

The machine moved in a quick and easy way. Watching it, I could almost have believed it was a real spider. Next to it, even the amazing fighting machines seemed stiff.

Now I also saw a Martian up close. The large round body was really its head. It had two eyes but no nose. Around the mouth were two sets of long, waving hands. There were eight hands in each set.

We know now that a Martian was mostly just a brain. It did not need to sleep. It did not eat, but it did take blood from animals or from people to put into its own body. This may sound awful, but we eat meat from animals, don't we?

So the Martians were little more than brains, with different kinds of machines to help them move around and do what they needed to do. The machine that looked like a spider seemed more like a living thing than the Martians did.

More Martians

COMPREHENSION CHECK

Choose the best answer.

1. The author and his cowardly friend were in an empty house. They were hiding from
   ___a. the world.
   ___b. their wives.
   ___c. the black smoke.
   ___d. a group of robbers.

2. The author was very worried about
   ___a. his brother.
   ___b. his wife.
   ___c. his neighbors.
   ___d. his cowardly friend.

3. When the black smoke had disappeared, the author left the house
   ___a. to find his wife.
   ___b. to find his brother.
   ___c. to buy some food.
   ___d. to get to the coast and get out of the country.

4. The cowardly man did not want to leave the house. He finally left with the author because
   ___a. he liked his company.
   ___b. the author had all the food.
   ___c. the author owned a boat.
   ___d. he was afraid to be alone.

5. As they walked, the author and the coward were careful
   ___a. not to step on the grass.
   ___b. to hide from their neighbors.
   ___c. to hide from the Martians.
   ___d. not to eat up all their food.

6. At another house the author and the coward were eating, when
   ___a. the owners of the house came back and threw them out.
   ___b. the Martians began to break all the windows.
   ___c. the Martians blew up the house.
   ___d. another Thing from Mars had crashed nearby.

7. Peeking through a hole in the house, the author and the coward saw a new machine that looked like a
   ___a. spider.
   ___b. rabbit.
   ___c. turtle.
   ___d. raccoon.

8. The Martians did not need to sleep or eat. But they did need
   ___a. candy.
   ___b. blood.
   ___c. exercise.
   ___d. coffee.

9. Another name for this story could be
   ___a. "Sitting Ducks."
   ___b. "Attack of the Spiders."
   ___c. "Hiding from the Martians."
   ___d. "No Brains."

10. This story is mainly about
    ___a. two men who try to find their way to safety.
    ___b. two men who do not get along with each other.
    ___c. a man who always worries about his wife.
    ___d. why Martians drink blood.

Check your answers with the key on page 67.

More Martians

VOCABULARY CHECK

blood	discover	dust	fifth	spider	stiff

I. Sentences to Finish

Fill in the blank in each sentence with the correct key word from the box above.

1. Bill killed the _____ when he stepped on it.

2. I couldn't turn my head because my neck was _____ .

3. The doctor gave Joseph a _____ test yesterday.

4. On my _____ try, the ball went in the basket.

5. It took hours to clean the _____ out of the old barn.

6. Someday we might _____ life on other worlds.

II. Word Search

All the words from the box above are hidden in the puzzle below. They may be written from left to right, or up and down. As you find each word, put a circle around it. One word, that is not a key word, has been done for you.

```
F  I  F  D  E  T  S  O
S  I  F  F  B  U  P  V
D  I  S  T  L  S  I  E
A  F  L  O  O  P  D  S
D  I  S  C  O  V  E  R
U  F  T  X  D  A  R  K
S  T  I  F  B  L  O  S
T  H  F  D  I  S  C  O
F  I  F  T  E  D  U  S
```

Check your answers with the key on page 71.

This page may be reproduced for classroom use.

Hiding Out

PREPARATION

Key Words

blade   (blād)   thing used to cut
The cook used a large <u>blade</u> to cut the meat.

careless   (ker´ lis, kar´ lis)   not careful
She lost the book because she was <u>careless</u>.

cause   (kôz)   reason why something happens
The <u>cause</u> of the excitement was a kitten caught in a tree.

throat   (thrōt)   front of the neck; the passage from the mouth to the stomach or lungs
After you chew your food, it goes down your <u>throat</u>.

wall   (wôl)   part of a room or building
Let's hang this picture on the <u>wall</u>.

weep   (wēp)   cry
People <u>weep</u> when sad things happen.

Hiding Out

Necessary Words

companion (kəm pan´ yən) one who goes along with another; one who shares in what another is doing
> *The two men had been <u>companions</u> since they were young boys.*

Hiding Out

We were both curious to see what was happening,
but the opening in the wall was only large enough for one to look out.

Preview: 1. Read the name of the story.
             2. Look at the picture.
             3. Read the sentence under the picture.
             4. Read the first two paragraphs of the story.
             5. Then answer the following question.

You learned from your preview that the author and his companion
___ a. wanted to give up.
___ b. complained all the time.
___ c. were running out of food.
___ d. were not in any danger.

Turn to the Comprehension Check on page 52 for the right answer.

Now read the story.

Read to find out what happens to the cowardly man.

Hiding Out

The small opening in the wall was only large enough for one to look out. It soon was a cause of trouble between me and my companion. We feared that the Martians would hear us or see us. We could not be careless, yet we both were curious to see what they were doing. So we pushed and kicked at each other for a chance to look.

The two of us did not get along at all. I tried to think of a plan to save us, but all he did was weep and complain. He ate more than I did, and he did not listen when I warned him that we would soon run out of food. As the days went by, the careless way he acted made our danger even greater.

Looking out through the opening, we saw that the Martians were bringing people to this place. On our third day there, I saw a Martian take blood from one of the people. I wanted so much to get away from there that I started to dig my way out. But the digging made too much noise, and I had to give it up.

The other man and I had been in the house about six days when I caught him in the kitchen taking food. After that, I divided up all the food we had left and would not let him take more than his share. For the next two days he did

little but weep and try to fight me. He began talking louder and louder, which was a cause of great worry for me. I was afraid that the Martians would hear him.

By the next day, much of what he was saying didn't even make sense. He began to shout, and I knew they would hear him through the wall. Then he stood up and headed for the door, still shouting.

I put out my hand and felt a blade for cutting meat that was hanging on the kitchen wall. In a flash I was after him, fierce with fear. Before he could reach the door, I caught him. I turned the blade of the meat cutter away from him and hit him with the handle. He fell to the ground and lay there.

Suddenly I heard a noise outside. The long arm of one of the Martian machines was coming through the hole!

I ran into a little room where coal was kept and pulled the door shut. I could hear the Martian pulling on something heavy in the kitchen. Peeking out, I saw that it had hold of the man who had shared my stay in this awful place.

I shut the door again and tried to cover myself with coal. From the kitchen, I heard the sounds of the Martian's arm moving about. Then I heard it stop. It had

found the door! And it knew how to open it!

Into the small coal room came the Martian's arm. It looked like an elephant's trunk, waving from side to side. It touched the wall. It touched the coal. Once it even touched my boot!

At last the arm picked something up, maybe a piece of coal, and went out of the room. I heard it moving around and breaking things in the kitchen. Then the house was silent again.

I did not dare come out of the coal room all the rest of that day. My throat burned for a drink of water. When I did go to the kitchen, I found that the Martian had taken every bit of food.

The next few days were terrible. I was hungry all the time. I had only a little bit of dirty water to drink, and my throat hurt badly.

Then a little dog came barking at the opening in the wall. I listened for the Martians, but all was quiet. They were gone at last!

Outside, the world had changed. Everywhere I looked, a strange red plant was growing. It seemed to cover everything.

Hiding Out

COMPREHENSION CHECK

Choose the best answer.

1. The author and his companion
   ___a. got along very well with each other.
   ___b. did not get along at all.
   ___c. were careless people.
   ___d. were very much alike.

2. The careless way the companion acted
   ___a. made the author feel comfortable.
   ___b. made the author feel wonderful.
   ___c. amused the author.
   ___d. placed them in great danger.

3. The author tried to
   ___a. dig his way out of the house.
   ___b. escape through the roof.
   ___c. escape through a window.
   ___d. get out through a back door.

4. The author gave up digging because
   ___a. he got very tired.
   ___b. it made him very thirsty.
   ___c. he was making too much noise.
   ___d. he broke his shovel.

5. Hearing a noise outside, the author hid. He watched as one of the Martians
   ___a. entered the house through a kitchen window.
   ___b. came through the front door.
   ___c. drank a cup of coffee.
   ___d. took hold of his companion.

6. What do you think the Martians were going to do with this man?
   ___a. Eat him for breakfast
   ___b. Drink his blood
   ___c. Send him home
   ___d. Send him to Mars

7. When the author left the coal room and went into the kitchen,
   ___a. he fixed himself something to eat.
   ___b. he found that all the food was gone.
   ___c. he found blood all over the floor.
   ___d. he found all his dishes broken.

8. When the author finally went outside, he found
   ___a. his dead companion.
   ___b. a hungry little dog.
   ___c. his wife.
   ___d. red plants growing everywhere.

9. Another name for this story could be
   ___a. "Days and Nights of Terror."
   ___b. "Silent Night."
   ___c. "Giving Up."
   ___d. "Afternoon Adventure."

10. This story is mainly about
    ___a. two men who argue day and night.
    ___b. two men who struggle to stay alive.
    ___c. two men who were hungry and couldn't find food.
    ___d. Martians who drink blood.

Check your answers with the key on page 67.

Hiding Out

VOCABULARY CHECK

blade	careless	cause	throat	wall	weep

I. Sentences to Finish

Fill in the blank in each sentence with the correct key word from the box above.

1. The _____ way he drove the car frightened me.

2. The hot sun will _____ the snowman to melt.

3. Joe's _____ hurt, so he went to the doctor.

4. Mom cut her finger on the _____ of the knife.

5. I _____ when I see a real sad movie.

6. The picture fell off the _____ and broke.

II. Mixed-up Words

First, unscramble the letters in Column A to spell out the key words. Then, match the key words with the right meaning in Column B by drawing a line.

Column A

1. ewep _____

2. scareels _____

3. dlabe _____

4. athrot _____

5. lawl _____

6. scuea _____

Column B

a. the passage from the mouth to the stomach or lungs

b. cry

c. thing used to cut

d. part of a room or building

e. reason why something happens

f. not careful

Check your answers with the key on page 71.

This page may be reproduced for classroom use.

53

The World Outside

PREPARATION

Key Words

ant	(ant)	tiny animal *If you want to see an <u>ant</u>, try having a picnic.*
dream	(drēm)	thoughts or pictures that happen while you sleep; an idea or a wish *Last night I had a <u>dream</u> about a funny clown.*
inn	(in)	place where people away from home can sleep and get food *We stayed at an <u>inn</u> one night on our way to my uncle's house.*
lonely	(lōn´ lē)	sad at being alone *She was <u>lonely</u> when her friends were away.*
none	(nun)	not any *He wanted an apple, but there were <u>none</u> left.*
tunnel	(tun´ l)	a kind of long hole which passes under ground *We drove through a <u>tunnel</u> that went under the hill.*

The World Outside

Necessary Words

germs	(jürmz)	very tiny animals that can make people, animals, or plants not feel well

Wash your hands to get rid of <u>germs</u> that might give you a cold.

The World Outside

As I hunted for something to eat, I found the red plants everywhere.

Preview: 1. Read the name of the story.
2. Look at the picture.
3. Read the sentence under the picture.
4. Read the first three paragraphs of the story.
5. Then answer the following question.

You learned from your preview that the Martians
___ a. liked to eat plants.
___ b. liked to eat red meat.
___ c. had gone back to Mars.
___ d. had taken over everything.

Turn to the Comprehension Check on page 58 for the right answer.

Now read the story.

Read to find out where the Martians are headed.

The World Outside

For some time I stood outside, amazed by the strange red plants. All that time I was in the house I had not known what was happening to the world. Now it looked like something you would see in a dream.

I knew that the red plants must have come from Mars. That thought gave me a very strange feeling. I felt as an ant must feel, without power, no longer a master of my own world. The Martians had taken over everything.

As I hunted for something to eat, I found the red plant everywhere. In places it was a high as my neck. It grew both on land and in water, filling the rivers.

In the end, the red plants died as quickly as they had grown. On Earth we have many germs, and our plants have ways to fight them. The red plants could not fight the germs, and so they died.

I kept hoping that I would meet other people, but I saw none. And I did not see any Martians. I thought that the Martians must have killed everyone else around here. Now they might be doing the same thing in other lands.

That night I came to an inn at the top of a hill. I found a tiny bit of food there and, for the first time in many nights, I had a real bed to sleep in. But that was a terrible night.

I had never been so lonely. Thoughts of what might have happened to my wife frightened me and made me sad.

The next morning was bright and fine. When I left the inn, I did not really know where to go. I thought of heading for the town where I had left my wife, but I knew there was no chance of finding her there. I was very lonely for her and for the world of living people.

I had stopped to watch some frogs, when I got the feeling that someone was watching me. I turned to find a man standing there. He was dirty and covered with dust, as I was myself. But we soon recognized each other. It was the soldier I had met in my garden. We had lost each other during the fight with the Martians at the river.

Now he told me that the Martians had gone away toward London. He had seen none for five days, but there were bright lights in their camp every night. He believed that they had made a flying machine. With a flying machine, they could go all over the Earth.

"The Martians have won the war," he said. "It was like a war between men and ants. That's what we are now, just ants."

But the soldier had a plan. He told me he was digging a tunnel. Those of us who were still living would join together and live under the ground where the Martians couldn't find us. The soldier thought we could find ways to take over some of the Martians' machines. Then we would have a way to fight back.

I went with him to see the tunnel he had told me about. He said he had been working for a week, but it did not look like he had worked very hard. I could have made a tunnel that long in just one day.

I stayed with the soldier all that day. We ate a good meal, for he had found food in empty homes and stores. We worked a little on the tunnel. But I soon began to see that my friend liked to talk about his dream of fighting the Martians more than he liked to work.

That night I went outside and looked at the sky. I decided to go into London. There I had the best chance of finding out what the Martians were doing and what else might be happening in the world.

The World Outside

COMPREHENSION CHECK

Choose the best answer.

Preview Answer:
d. had taken over everything.

1. The red plants died quickly because
   ___a. they grew too fast.
   ___b. they grew too big.
   ___c. no one watered them.
   ___d. they couldn't fight the germs that made them sick.

2. The author, finding no one else around, thought that
   ___a. the Martians had killed everyone.
   ___b. everyone got away safely.
   ___c. everyone died of germs like the red plants.
   ___d. everyone was hiding.

3. When night came, the author found some food and a bed
   ___a. in the next town.
   ___b. at the soldiers' camp.
   ___c. at an inn.
   ___d. in a house by the river.

4. At the inn, the author
   ___a. slept soundly.
   ___b. did not get much sleep.
   ___c. had a frightening dream.
   ___d. had a restful evening.

5. The author was lonely for
   ___a. the world as it used to be.
   ___b. his wife.
   ___c. people.
   ___d. all of the above.

6. The author met a soldier who told him that
   ___a. the Martians had won the war.
   ___b. the Martians had gone back to Mars.
   ___c. all the Martians had died.
   ___d. he was leaving the city in his flying machine.

7. The soldier's plan was to
   ___a. dig a tunnel that would lead him out to sea.
   ___b. dig a tunnel to London.
   ___c. dig a tunnel and live under the ground.
   ___d. build better machines than the Martians had.

8. The author knew that the soldier's plan
   ___a. was a good idea.
   ___b. was an easy one.
   ___c. was too silly to think about.
   ___d. would never work.

9. Another name for this story could be
   ___a. "A New Earth."
   ___b. "The Martians' Flying Machines."
   ___c. "Lonely Dreams."
   ___d. "Digging Out."

10. This story is mainly about
   ___a. a man who was all alone in the world.
   ___b. the many germs found on Earth.
   ___c. a war between men and ants.
   ___d. how the Martians were changing a beautiful world into a horrible place.

Check your answers with the key on page 67.

This page may be reproduced for classroom use.

The World Outside

VOCABULARY CHECK

ant	dream	inn	lonely	none	tunnel

I. Sentences to Finish

Fill in the blank in each sentence with the correct key word from the box above.

1. We drove all day and stopped at an _____ to rest.

2. Sally felt very _____ when her best friend moved away.

3. _____ of the children would listen to the teacher.

4. The train passed under the mountains through a _____ .

5. At the family picnic, I found an _____ in my sandwich.

6. When you wake up from a bad _____ it's hard to fall asleep again.

II. Using the Words

On the lines below, write six of your own sentences using the key words from the box above. Use each word once, drawing a line under the key word.

1. _____

2. _____

3. _____

4. _____

5. _____

6. _____

Check your answers with the key on page 71.

After the War

PREPARATION

Key Words

alive	(ə līv´)	having life *Plants need water to keep them <u>alive</u>.*
bent	(bent)	not straight *The front of the bicycle got <u>bent</u> when it hit the fence.*
cousin	(kuz´ n)	the child of one's aunt or uncle *My aunt and uncle have a new baby, so I have a new little <u>cousin</u>.*
sick	(sik)	not well *I stayed home from school because I was <u>sick</u>.*
thin	(thin)	not fat or wide *He stays <u>thin</u> no matter how much he eats.*
wreck	(rek)	something that is broken and cannot be used *The house was a <u>wreck</u> after the storm.*

After the War

Necessary Words

groceries   (grō´ sər ēs)   items of food found in a store or home
Mother and I went shopping for <u>groceries</u>.

After the War

I felt like I was the only person alive in all of London.

Preview:	1. Read the name of the story.
	2. Look at the picture.
	3. Read the sentence under the picture.
	4. Read the first two paragraphs of the story.
	5. Then answer the following question.

You learned from your preview that the streets of London were

___ a. very noisy.

___ b. empty and silent.

___ c. covered with snow.

___ d. wet with rain.

Turn to the Comprehension Check on page 64 for the right answer.

Now read the story.

Read to find out what ends the war.

After the War

After I left the soldier, I started for London. The dust from the black smoke was everywhere. So were the red plants, but I noticed that a few were turning white. They were already sick and beginning to die.

The streets of London were empty and silent. It seemed that I was the only one alive in the whole city. Then I heard a strange noise, a terrible cry. "Ulla, ulla, ulla, ulla." It went on and on without stopping.

I was tired, hungry, and lonely. What was I doing here, all alone in this empty city? I found groceries and something to drink in a place that had been an inn. Then I fell asleep. When I woke again, the terrible sound was still in my ears. "Ulla, ulla, ulla, ulla."

I had not walked far, when I saw the Martian machine from which the sound came. I watched it for some time, but it did not move. It just stood there crying.

I turned away and soon came upon the wreck of another machine. This was one of those that looked like a spider. Now it lay here, bent and broken. A bit farther on, I saw another one of the tall machines with three legs. It just stood there, not moving or making any sound. But the cry from the first machine went on and on. "Ulla, ulla, ulla, ulla."

I was crossing a small bridge when the noise suddenly stopped. Everything was quiet. Now more than ever I felt that I was the only thing left alive.

By the next day, my courage had returned, and I found my way to the camp the Martians had made. I saw one of their machines with its long arms bent in a strange way. It was a wreck. There were other machines there, too, but nothing was moving, nothing at all.

The Martians were dead! They had gotten sick and died, killed by germs that their bodies could not fight, just as the red plants were being killed. Germs, tiny little germs, had saved our Earth from the Martians!

As I looked about, I saw that the germs had saved us just in time. For there was the flying machine the soldier had told me about. With that, the Martians would have taken over the whole world.

But now it was over. Those who were still alive would come back. We would repair all that had been burned and broken. Then I thought of my wife and our life together, a life that we would never have again.

Soon people did begin to come back. All of us were dressed in rags. We were dirty, thin, and hungry. Other countries sent bread, corn, and meat to help feed us. Now there were a few carts on the streets, but the horses that pulled them were as thin as the people.

I found out that free trains were running to take people back to their homes. So I came back at last to my own house. I hoped that somehow my wife and cousin might still be alive. I hoped that my wife had found her way back home.

But the house was empty and silent. Everything was exactly as I had left it almost four weeks ago, and I knew that no one had been there.

Then a strange thing happened. I thought I heard a voice saying, "It is no use. No one has been here." I hurried to the window and looked out. There, as amazed as I, stood my cousin and my wife!

We now know that there is life on other worlds. Maybe a day will come when the Martians will attack again. Maybe a day will come when we will build our own ships and travel to other worlds.

To me, nothing is more strange than to hold my wife's hand and to think that once we believed we would never see each other again.

After the War

COMPREHENSION CHECK

Choose the best answer.

1. In London, the author was found to be
   ___a. tired.
   ___b. hungry.
   ___c. lonely.
   ___d. all of the above.

2. He found something to eat and drink
   ___a. in a place that had been an inn.
   ___b. in a grocery store.
   ___c. in an old schoolhouse.
   ___d. in his brother's house.

3. He had not walked far, when he heard a strange sound that came from
   ___a. a passing train.
   ___b. a hole in the ground.
   ___c. the sick, red plants.
   ___d. one of the Martian machines.

4. A Martian inside one of the machines was crying because
   ___a. it wanted to go home.
   ___b. it was sick.
   ___c. it was hungry.
   ___d. it was lonely.

5. What caused the Martians to get sick and die?
   ___a. The red plants
   ___b. The soldiers' guns
   ___c. Germs
   ___d. The water

6. The tiny little germs had
   ___a. taken over the world.
   ___b. saved the world.
   ___c. cleaned up the Earth.
   ___d. brought harm to the Earth.

7. Now that the war was over, people returned home and
   ___a. tried to make new friends.
   ___b. tried to rebuild their lives.
   ___c. kept to themselves.
   ___d. locked their doors.

8. The author returned to his home where he found
   ___a. his wife and cousin.
   ___b. his wife and brother.
   ___c. his wife and sister.
   ___d. no one.

9. Another name for this story could be
   ___a. "The Silent City."
   ___b. "The Martians Go Home."
   ___c. "How the Earth was Saved."
   ___d. "Life on Mars."

10. This story is mainly about
    ___a. how the world was saved from the Martians.
    ___b. how the world had changed after the war.
    ___c. what life is like on other worlds.
    ___d. a man who finds his wife.

Check your answers with the key on page 67.

This page may be reproduced for classroom use.

After the War

VOCABULARY CHECK

| alive | bent | cousin | sick | thin | wreck |

I. Sentences to Finish

Fill in the blank in each sentence with the correct key word from the box above.

1. The drowning boy was still _____ when we pulled him from the river.

2. When we stay at Uncle Bob's house, I share a room with my _____ .

3. Jane was _____ and couldn't go to school.

4. It is a bad idea to go skating on _____ ice.

5. The strong man at the circus _____ the iron bar with his hands.

6. The car was a _____ after it hit the tree.

II. Making Sense of Sentences

Put a check next to YES if the sentence makes sense. Put a check next to NO if the sentence does not make sense.

1. The dog was found <u>alive</u> after it was killed. _____ YES _____ NO

2. It feels good to be <u>sick</u> with a cold. _____ YES _____ NO

3. Mother was not pleased to find the house a <u>wreck</u>. _____ YES _____ NO

4. A baby horse has very <u>thin</u> legs. _____ YES _____ NO

5. A <u>cousin</u> is your neighbor's child. _____ YES _____ NO

6. If something is <u>bent</u>, it is not straight. _____ YES _____ NO

Check your answers with the key on page 72.

This page may be reproduced for classroom use.

NOTES

COMPREHENSION CHECK ANSWER KEY
Lessons CTR 306-51 to CTR 306-60

LESSON NUMBER	QUESTION NUMBER										PAGE NUMBER
	1	2	3	4	5	6	7	8	9	10	
CTR C-51	a	d	b	c	a	c	(a)	b	△c	□a	10
CTR C-52	b	a	c	d	d	c	(a)	d	△a	□b	16
CTR C-53	b	d	c	a	a	(d)	d	(b)	△a	□c	22
CTR C-54	d	b	c	a	(c)	a	d	(a)	△b	□c	28
CTR C-55	b	c	b	a	d	d	(a)	c	△a	□d	34
CTR C-56	b	a	d	(c)	d	a	b	d	△d	□c	40
CTR C-57	c	b	(a)	(d)	c	d	a	b	△c	□a	46
CTR C-58	b	d	a	c	d	(b)	b	d	△a	□b	52
CTR C-59	d	a	c	(b)	d	a	c	(d)	△a	□d	58
CTR C-60	d	a	d	b	c	b	(b)	a	△c	□a	64

◯ = Inference (not said straight out, but you know from what is said)

△ = Another name for the story

□ = Main idea of the story

67

NOTES

VOCABULARY CHECK ANSWER KEY

Lessons CTR C-51 to CTR C-60

LESSON NUMBER		PAGE NUMBER

51 THE THING FROM MARS — 11

I.
1. flame
2. Earth
3. smoke
4. upon
5. war
6. space

II.
1. NO
2. YES
3. NO
4. NO
5. YES
6. YES

52 FRIDAY NIGHT — 17

I.
1. weight
2. Friday
3. heat
4. puff
5. alarm
6. ugly

II.
1. e
2. f
3. d
4. b
5. c
6. a

53 THE WAR BEGINS — 23

I.
1. body
2. metal
3. tower
4. huge
5. dead
6. cart

II.
1. huge
2. cart
3. tower
4. dead
5. metal
6. body
RIDDLE: hardly

VOCABULARY CHECK ANSWER KEY

Lessons CTR C-51 to CTR C-60

LESSON NUMBER   **PAGE NUMBER**

54 A TERRIBLE FIGHT   29

I.
1. crash
2. dawn
3. hundred
4. meal
5. women
6. direction

II.

```
        D
        A
        W
  H U N D R E D
        I
        R
        E
        C
        T
        I
        O
  W O M E N
      E
  C R A S H
      L
```

55 THE BLACK SMOKE   35

I.
1. Sunday
2. power
3. repair
4. event
5. probably
6. Monday

56 MY BROTHER'S ESCAPE   41

I.
1. ship
2. cloud
3. travel
4. courage
5. pale
6. coast

II.
1. b
2. d
3. f
4. a
5. c
6. e

VOCABULARY CHECK ANSWER KEY

Lessons CTR C-51 to CTR C-60

57 MORE MARTIANS   47

I.   1. spider
    2. stiff
    3. blood
    4. fifth
    5. dust
    6. discover

II.

```
F  I  F  D  E  T  S  O
S  I  F  F  B  U  P  V
D  I  S  T  L  S  I  E
A  F  L  O  O  P  D  S
D  I  S  C  O  V  E  R
U  F  T  X  D  A  R  K
S  T  I  F  B  L  O  S
T  H  I  F  D  I  S  C  O
F  I  F  T  E  D  U  S
```

58 HIDING OUT   53

I.   1. careless
    2. cause
    3. throat
    4. blade
    5. weep
    6. wall

II.   1. weep, b
    2. careless, f
    3. blade, c
    4. throat, a
    5. wall, d
    6. cause, e

59 THE WORLD OUTSIDE   59

I.   1. inn
    2. lonely
    3. None
    4. tunnel
    5. ant
    6. dream

VOCABULARY CHECK ANSWER KEY

Lessons CTR C-51 to CTR C-60

LESSON
NUMBER

PAGE
NUMBER

60 **AFTER THE WAR**

65

I. 1. alive
   2. cousin
   3. sick
   4. thin
   5. bent
   6. wreck

II. 1. NO
   2. NO
   3. YES
   4. YES
   5. NO
   6. YES